A Nest
Full of Stars

A Nest Full of Stars

POEMS BY
James Berry

WITH PICTURES BY
Ashley Bryan

Greenwillow Books
An Imprint of HarperCollins*Publishers*

Amistad

For Anita
—J.B.

For an artist and dear friend,
Rose Russo
—A.B.

A Nest Full of Stars
Text copyright © 2002 by James Berry
Illustrations copyright © 2004 by Ashley Bryan

First published in Great Britain in 2002 by Macmillan Children's Books,
a division of Pan Macmillan Limited.
First published in the United States in 2004 by Greenwillow Books,
an imprint of HarperCollins Publishers.
Amistad is an imprint of HarperCollins Publishers, Inc.
The right of James Berry to be identified as the author
of this book has been asserted by him.

The text of this book is set in Korinna.

Library of Congress Cataloging-in-Publication Data
Berry, James.
A nest full of stars : poems / by James Berry ; pictures by Ashley Bryan.
p.   cm.
"Greenwillow Books."
Summary: A collection of poems reflecting Caribbean culture including
"Old men called Arawak," "Woods whisperings," and "Not one weak day."
ISBN 0-06-052747-1 (trade). ISBN 0-06-052748-X (lib. bdg.)
1. Caribbean Area—Juvenile poetry. 2. Children's poetry, Jamaican.
[1. Caribbean Area—Poetry. 2. Jamaican poetry.] I. Bryan, Ashley, ill. II. Title.
PR9265.9.B47 N47 2004   821'.914—dc21   2002032176

1 2 3 4 5 6 7 8 9 10
First American Edition

 Greenwillow Books

CONTENTS

Foreword

I was born and brought up in a coastal and rural Jamaican village in the 1930s. Though I was schooled with literature from Great Britain, the written stories that really influenced me were mostly Old Testament Bible stories.

We had nothing like a school library or easy access to any public library. And, since they were beyond my parents' purchasing power, children's stories were practically absent from my childhood home. Yet I loved being the celebrated little marvel I was, able to read somewhere between the ages of three and four and a special favorite at my village nursery.

I started attending writers' workshops in my mid-twenties in London. Eventually I developed a strong yearning to write poems based on forms and influences drawn from everyday Caribbean language and culture. My problem was that I had not found any examples I could draw on that represented the subjects and language sounds that had given me such pleasure during my childhood and teenage life.

At school in Jamaica, our Caribbean Creole speech had become established as "Bad Talk." We were made to memorize poems like Eliza Cook's "Try Again," about Robert the Bruce, King of Scotland, and the spider. We also sang poems like Ben Jonson's seventeenth-century "Drink to Me Only with Thine Eyes." At that time there was nothing called a "Caribbean poem." Yet my yearning to celebrate these sounds survived to changed times.

You will see my interpretation of Caribbean language sounds here, in echoes that have resurfaced from my school days, poems like "Caribbean Playground Song," "Old Men Called Arawak," "Donkey Story," "Doubtful Sayings," and others. Poems such as "Gobble-Gobble Rap," and "Getting Bigger Rap" merely try to express a more extended urban sound.

The poems "From My Sister's Secret Notebook" are here to celebrate our only sister among five boys. The events in her poem "A Nest Full of Stars" happened in our childhood. In our family each child had a particular hen or two, and a pig and goat or two, that were his or her own to look after. These animals helped to yield some money toward buying a school textbook or a piece of clothing. Our ownership of them generated competition, rivalry, and a sense of failure or success. To my sister, her hen was sensational. Her hen had been amazingly secretive, while being successful in providing a nest full of eggs.

James Berry

A Nest
Full of Stars

Everyday Feelings

Everyday Feelings

Terror sets off a shock stuff
in your voice
that makes it screamy, squeaky, gruff.

Laughing has a twitch switch
in your tummy and toes
that dances freckles on your nose.

Not One Weak Day

Monday comes—
it is that mighty shock
of a mind-jogging day.

Tuesday comes—
it is that tuning in and getting on
of a no-choosing day.

Wednesday comes—
it is that walled-in work
of a middle-week day.

Thursday comes—
it is that tough exploration trip
of a tumbling-over-bumpy-waves day.

Friday comes—
it is that fattening feast
of a frying-up and fast-food day.

Saturday comes—
it is that shop, swim, play
of a swish-about day.

Sunday comes—
it is that special sparkler
of a little Christmas Day.

Sometimes

Sometimes
I help with getting supper.
Other times
I help with the grass cutter.

Sometimes
I help with classroom clear-ups.
Other times
I'm not blameless over a trip-up.

Sometimes
I act soft and woolly.
Other times
I stand up to a bully.

Sometimes
I am hairy, tough, scary.
Other times
I am just a well-washed and brushed,
sweet-smelly, cutey baby.

Big Page Writer

Just carrying on writing
like a hardworking explorer
I suddenly have a full half page
making me a real big page writer.

Voices of alphabet shapes, welcome
like eyeballs, birds' footprints, twigs, pebbles
from my head down through my pen
to be talking squiggles.

Flat out, writing, exploring, I get
marked: CAN DO BETTER, or, just, GOOD:
when, all silent—full of great voices—
my big half page holds a mighty *magic* mood.

Mood Manager

Come on, LAZY MOOD,
let me stay in bed
all day, reading and eating.

Come on, SCARY MOOD,
see a monster make me scream
something truly awful.

Come on, BIG BOLD MOOD,
make me beat up
a pensioner's burglar.

Come on, SAD MOOD,
stop saying remember:
Grandma is dead forever.

Come on, WILLING MOOD,
have me pushing home
a weary wheelchair person.

Come on, MISER MOOD,
make me manage without
touching my pocket money.

Come on, GUESSING MOOD,
make me guess my wished-for
birthday gift, there parceled up.

Come on, TICKLED MOOD,
keep me feeling trumps
answering that quiz correctly.

Come on, LUCKY MOOD,
make it a lottery win
houseful of money today.

Come on, NOISY MOOD,
make me holler, shouting:
I passed the test!

Sly Force Waiting

1 knew that horrible
hunger strength of my jaws,
when I last bit my tongue.

I knew that dreadful
ducking hold of water,
when I fell into a swimming pool.

I knew that swallowing
slide of a pit, when I dropped
into a beach sand hole.

The Adding-Up of Birthdays

People say:
You shove in your food like a spade
yet can't even slice bread straight.

You gawp at others' heaped plates
yet always fall just trying to skate.

You can't even get yourself up, awake
without even having stayed up late.

You are always the one with mucked-up hair
at home, at school, everywhere.

You are the only one to walk and not run
and, that one, with shoelaces flapping, undone.

I say:
I have my great hope in that special day
which every year adds on *another* BIRTHDAY!

Somewhere! Somewhere!

Take me somewhere—
to the circus:
to spinning wheels and noisy bells.
Blazing stripes and streaks of yells.
Seeing swingers and clowns
round and round ceilings and walls.

Take me somewhere—
to the fair:
make me dither, jump, slither.
Make me slide and glide on feet and side.
Let me leap through hoops
and feel I move with pounding hooves.

Take me somewhere—
to a big street carnival:
finding drummers and bright dancers.
Getting my mouth all fishy, meaty,
peppery, spicy, buttery, sugary,
while music and revelry make me giddy.

Take me somewhere—
to wide-open countryside.
Let me redden and blacken
my tongue with berries and cherries.
Let me skip with a flip in a trip.
Take me somewhere.

Special Is Special

A special time can happen
so sudden
like unexpected win
of the hardest race.

A special time can bring
great friendships
carrying a trophy
and a chocolate cake for you.

A special time comes
and makes your stomach chuckle
with every good time
shining there on your face.

Fireworks

Bang after bang tosses out
star and sunlit pieces
in a lit-up shower, drifting down.

In a slow party dance
meshed in bright shapes
of glowing lacework, like

necklaces, branches, arrows,
all drift down in
flame pieces, rain sparkled.

A fantastic Christmas tree of space
disappears before your eyes—
making you know the saddest good-bye.

At the Showing-Off Event

Centipedes all say: Watch numberless
needle legs together, walking.

Snakes all say: Watch how piles
of coiled ropes come alive!

Dogs all say: Even a playful bark is
terror to thieves hiding. Dogs, come on,
for one minute, *let's bark something crazy!*

Mother birds tell baby birds: No!
No parading for you.
You need weeks to get dressed.

Wind says: Trees, let's work up
hard windy weather—now!

Child Member of
Parliament Manifesto

*W*hy are all days not fun days?
Nobody ever said: Let's get
work all out of the week!
Let's extract Monday to Friday!

Nobody ever said: Let's keep
only Saturday and Sunday!
Make playtime full time!
Make chocolate cake free!

Nobody ever said: Let's take
trouble all out of the week,
saving only Saturday and Sunday.
Here is my new children's manifesto.

People Equal

Some people shoot up tall.
Some hardly leave the ground at all.
          Yet—people equal. Equal.

One voice is a sweet mango.
Another is a nonsugar tomato.
          Yet—people equal. Equal.

Some people rush to the front.
Others hang back, feeling they can't.
          Yet—people equal. Equal.

Hammer some people, you meet a wall.
Blow hard on others, they fall.
          Yet—people equal. Equal.

One person will aim at a star.
For another, a hilltop is *too far*.
          Yet—people equal. Equal.

Some people get on with their show.
Others never get on the go.
          Yet—people equal. Equal.

Wild Whistling Woman

*W*ild whistling woman whistles up
windy weather.

Windy weather whistles up
wrecking water working.

Wrecking water working whistles up
wettest workless Wednesday.

Wettest workless Wednesday whistles up
wild waterways of welcome water.

Skeleton Sisters

Seven skeleton sisters all slowly
swallowed seven small, scrappy suppers.
And, Sunday-fed, soothed and satisfied,
each sister sang and sang her sweetest,
till sisters all sighed softly
and seemed ever so slightly swelled.

Gobble-Gobble Rap

Me do a whispa and a big shout
with a meat-and-a-sweet mouth
like a nonmeat, nonfish, puddn mouth
which is—a sleeper-waker, want-it-want-it mouth
which is—a take-it, break-it, eater mouth
which is—a gobble-gobble mouth.

Me do a whispa and a big shout
with an oily-oily, salty-pepper mouth
like any seafood, wing-food, ground-food mouth
which is—a want-more-now, want-more-now mouth
which is—a chopper-chopper, swallow-down mouth
which is—a gobble-gobble mouth.

Me do a whispa and a big shout
with a bony-and-a-fleshy-meaty mouth
like a buttered-up, creamed-up, oiled-up mouth
which is—a smile-and-smile, fries-and-fish mouth
which is—a loud, bossy-bossy mouth
which is—a gobble-gobble mouth.

Me do a whispa and a big shout
with a bun-and-cake and ice-cream mouth
like a shopping for a cupboard mouth
which is—a mouthy, eat-eat, noisy mouth
which is—a break-it-up, bite-it-up mouth
which is—a gobble-gobble mouth.

Me do a whispa and a big shout
with a pie, chocolate, and apple mouth
like any chatty-chatty, suck-sweet mouth
which is—an on-and-off, laugh-and-laugh mouth
which is—a gimme-gimme-more mouth
which is—a gobble-gobble mouth.

Me do a whispa and a big shout
with always that ready mouth about
like even that slurper-burper mouth
which is—a raver-craver, seeker mouth
which is—a singer and kissy-kissy mouth
which is—a gobble-gobble mouth
        which is—a gobble-gobble mouth.

Together

Together

I love it when we play
cricket or football
or sit and watch a game on TV.

Best of all
I love it when we swing together
and never stop
talking and laughing together
while we meet, all
passing each other on two swings
fitted to the same frame.

Then we go and buy
and eat ice cream slowly.
Yet, best of all
I love it when we swing together
talking and laughing, all
when passing each other.

The Quarrel

Jan and Gemma quarreled.
Gemma spoke about Jan's dog
as "only a mongrel."

Jan said, "If not really
nasty, that was unkind."

Gemma said, "Mongrel is
neither nasty nor unkind."

"Yes," Jan insisted.
"Mongrel is not a kind word.
Especially when
'only' is attached to it."

"Perhaps," Gemma said. "But
not *terrible, terrible,* is it?"

Jan said, "Call my dog
a 'mixed breed,' that is fine.
But—not 'only a mongrel.'"

Gemma said, "All right, Jan.
Suppose—I give you a fudge."

Jan said, "That would be friendly.
Especially—if 'sorry'
is written on it, in ink.

"And you give me another
one, to give back to you.
With 'sorry' on it in ink."

"Splendid," Gemma said. "Splendid."
Silent, for a little while,
both girls ate a fudge, carefully.

One Hand Washes the Other

*W*e lick same stick of ice cream.
We tickle each other to screams.

Just as each catches the ball from each
we leap the other's back with a touch.

Knowing each one's hating and loving
we rush with whispers to our hiding.

We get buried in sand together.
We sing with recordings together.

We blow that one lucky-dip whistle.
We share our one used tissue.

Like two head-to-tail horses standing in rain
one hand washes the other again and again.

Ball Gone Dialogue for Six

"Go and get the ball,"
                    (Nick shouts.)
"It's gone over the wall,"
                    (Ken says.)
"Sure, it's gone over the wall!"
                    (Nate says.)
"That Rottweiler is there,"
                    (Ken says.)
"Go on. Forget your fear,"
                    (Nick says.)
"I'll put the ladder down,"
                    (Kate says.)
"Yes. Put the ladder down,"
                    (Elton says.)
"My leg'll get hacked,"
                    (Ken says.)
"Tell leg: Drag the dog back,"
                    (Nate says.)
"Go and get the ball!"
                    (Nick shouts.)
"You go and get the ball!"
                    (Kate insists.)
"Don't you dare climb my wall!"
                    (Mr. Eflock says.)
"Here. I'm throwing *back* your ball."

Bowler's Talk to Himself
Walking Back to His Run-Up

*W*hat? What shall I send him?
Send him your corker of a yorker.
But—he's such a swift pouncer.

What? What shall I send him?
Bowler—bowl your ball.
But—he's such a stonewall.

What? What shall I send him?
Send him his ticket.
But—how he blocks up his wicket!

What? What shall I send him?
Have him dispatched.
But—my last ball was thrashed.

What? What shall I send him?
Know it—he said his last prayer.
But—think of his stored power!

What? What shall I send him?
Send him an out-swinger.
But—he's such a rapid blaster!

What? What shall I send him?
Bowler—bowl your ball.
But—he's hardest, hardest, to fall.

What? What shall I send him?
Chuck him your corker of a yorker.
Got him! Told you I'd make him a goner!

bowler: in cricket, similar to a pitcher in baseball

A Particular Time
at Our House

A Particular Time at Our House

Sweet-smelling, my dad shaves and sings.
My mum tries on different earrings.
Brother does a silly, tongue-twisting rap.
Our cat's curled up in my straw hat.
Our dog touches me with a paw.
Outside, loudly, a crow goes *caw!*

Dad's Night Voice

Why does my dad snore and snore
so? Sometimes I see it is
to have his roar filling
the house, even when he sleeps.

Smiling, sometimes I see
his snore is a croaking frog
with a bad cold, which has
taken over Dad's head.

Sometimes I wonder if he is
trying to start up the crowing
of distant roosters, as a boy said
his granddad's snoring used to do.

Other times, I see it is an old
car Dad's managed to get going
oddly, that shuts off only when
Mum shoves him, to sleep on his side.

Mum? Who Is My Mum?

One stuck with us, as endless worker.
And what a good job she's lots older.

She shouts: You are such a dreadful mess—
worse than a young bird dropped from a nest!

Yet, Mum makes the frying-up sizzle
and sees hungry faces change to a dazzle.

We push Mum, she's cool. She's patient.
She's healthy, wealthy, super-efficient.

But bowl Mum your very slowest ball—
Mum's great swipe does her wicket's downfall.

Seeing Mum really ill in bed
in silence, I know, I evenly cut the bread.

In Mum's apron, I'm boss of cooker,
TV, washing machine, vacuum cleaner.

Not Sharing

My sister stays on her new bicycle.
It has parts shining like silver.
The wheel tires are black.
The seat leather is dark brown.
My sister cleans her bicycle minutely.
She rides it round and round our garden.
She rides it up and down our street.
My sister is never tired
of her new bicycle. If she was, ever,
I might just get a ride on it.

Right Mix Like Water

Dad says, like H_2O, you
only need right input in
right order to have success
in anything you do.

I watched Dad and Mum
to see exactly how,
each time, they drove our car.

Nobody looking, I started
up the car and drove it
straight out of the garage.

Hard as I tried, I
could not reverse the car
back into the garage.

I switched it off.
I tiptoed upstairs.
I played my music loudest.

Then I saw Mum thought
Dad moved the car. I wished
and wished Dad thought
Mum had moved it.

Hearing

I lie in bed.
Sounds of a distant train passing
make me feel
at home and snug.

I walk in a woodland lane.
Song of a blackbird high up
makes me feel
accompanied.

I sit, looking out over the sea.
Sounds of high and flattened waves
make me hear
wind in hilly trees.

Eyes on the Time

When I travel in a train
and I want other passengers
to look at their watches,

I get my mum and dad
to mumble something to themselves
a little loudly, then look
at their watches with purpose.

Then I just sit back pop-eyed,
counting how many people do
look at their watches.

Going-Away Haiku

Boats and bikes roof-racked—
only stop, ice cream—aren't we
off on holiday!

Postcard Poem: Solo

Mum, you needn't have worried one bit.
I traveled fine, fine, solo. Carried
in steelbird belly of music shows.
I ate two passengers' pudding twice.
Nibbled nothings nutty and chocolaty.
Sipped cool Cokes. Had more nibbles.
All over mountain after mountain.
Over different oceans. Over
weird clouds, like snow hills
with trails of straggly shapes
drifting, searching. And strangers
talked—Germans going on big-fish hunt,
Italians to ride glass-bottomed boat,
a Dane to do snorkeling. Then, Mum,
I hopped from steelbird belly, down among
sun-roasted people of a palm-tree place.
Welcome to Jamaica, voices called out.
Whole family hugged a sweating me
and took me off. Other exotics
got collected up in cars and coaches
to be naked on beaches, while
steelbird stood there shiny-ready
for more come-and-go trips.

Sand-Seller Sam

Stuck to the seaside hut sides,
empty sacks had selling slogans for sand:

SAND-SELLER SPREADS THE SAND
OVER STONY-SIDE SEASIDE.

SAWDUST SOFTNESS OF SAM-SAND, ONLY
SEVEN POUNDS SEVENTY PENCE A SPREAD.

BE THE SEASIDE SMOOTHIE
SOAKING UP SEA, SUN, AND SAND SMOOTHLY.

SEE SANDCASTLE VILLAGE OF SAM-SAND—
SCENIC, SECURE, SUNNED.

GET SETTLED SAND-WALLOWING—
FOR NO-SCHOOL SEA-SIDING!

SAWDUST SOFTNESS OF SAM-SAND, ONLY
SEVEN POUNDS SEVENTY PENCE A SPREAD.

SAM-SAND! SAM-SAND! SAM-SAND!

From My Sister's
Secret Notebook

Earthworm and Fish

Like a gown, it wears the ground
and in there it is found.
Outside, it wiggles and squirms.
        It is a naked earthworm.

Like a gown, it wears water
and shares that living quarters.
Outside, soon, fish is dead.
        Is open air like heaven to a fish?

Seashell

Shell at my ear—
come share how I hear
busy old sea in whispers.

Moans rise from ancient depths
in ocean sighs
like crowds of ghost monsters.

Waves lash and fall—
in roars and squalls
with all a mystery *ahhh*!

Spider Ropes

Alone in woods, I hunt
for pretty leaves dropped
and smooth stones like marbles.

I come back feeling
my face is well laced
with leaves and spiders' webs.

Water Carrying

The stream gargles; beside it
bamboo trees brush their leaves
to a whispering, like silk.

I sit in the shadow, on
a broad flat stone, watching
cows and horses come and drink.

I listen to the crisscross
of bird songs, in a world
of clear, hot sunshine.

I fill my bucket. I go through
the turnstile. With my sandaled feet
I walk along my gravel road.

In the Hills, at Puppah's Food Cultivation Land

*W*e had just eaten roast corn
and coconut, when I saw
a mosquito, on my arm, full
of my blood showing through
its ballooned little body.

I knew I would squash it,
splashing my arm with blood. But
as I began to raise my hand
the brute insect lifted off,
swaying with overload.

Running, I followed the flying
thief. It zoomed up, away
into a tree branch. It was gone.

Trapped

I only tried to set the trap
and didn't expect it to snap.
Feeling such a sudden whack
I endured such a lonely shock.
        I only tried to set the trap
        and didn't expect it to snap.

Flash of trap—with its spiked catcher—
fastened down my every finger.
Oh, how I cried and softly cried!
Getting so hurt, I could've died.
        I only tried to set the trap
        to catch that banana-eating rat:
        and didn't expect it to snap.

Self-Supporting Village Pet

A striking cat, Bridie is all
of a black coat with a white splash, like
a scarf, round her shoulders, down to chest.
And what Bridie feels for, Bridie goes for.

Having a crave, Bridie is seen
to leap up and catch a bird flying
past her: paws grasping it as if
they were small hands, quick and firm.

Her knowing correct, Bridie hunts
from a rock in the village stream,
to leave only fish bones there
on top of her stone table.

People see Bridie eating meat
and not know where she gets it.
People see her eating fish at
the seaside, ten minutes' walk away.

Up in an avocado tree, crouching
between the limbs, lying down, or sitting,
Bridie ignores people watching
and simply holds her fruit, eating it.

Now, a kitten hanging from her jaws,
Bridie carries her new babies,
one by one, inside
to nurse them under her owners' bed.

Estate Cowman

The cowman passes you and hits you
with smells of cows, tar, disinfectant,
and stale rum drinking.

The cowman is a nasty-mouth man.
He herds the estate cows
with cracks of whip
and thunderclaps of swearwords
that pop a blue litter of lights
like bangers of fireworks clappers.

The cowman is a nasty-mouth man.
Any wonder—when he herds the cows
to dip them against lice and ticks—
passing mothers walk with hands
over their children's ears?

Everyday Music

All a mix together
village sounds make my music
   with horses' hooves clop-clopping
   flock of hens cackling
   woodchopping echoing
   a donkey hee-hawing
   roosters all around crowing.

All a mix together
village sounds make my music
   with wind and rain rushing
   our flooded gulley babbling
   birds all around singing
   a lonely cow mooing
   rolling sea land drumming.

All a mix together
village sounds make my music
   with fighting dogs yelping
   birds in trees twittering
   a lonely goat bleating
   hidden ground doves cooing
   hidden mongoose shrieking.

Thinking Before I Sleep

It's good seeing how—
like jaws biting into food
and scissors cutting into paper—
legs move, one after the other.

It's good seeing how—
like leaves falling—
birds flutter down
with open wings to settle.

It's good seeing how—
like a road or a foot track—
water makes its own way, over
and between hills and rocks,
to flow on, in its own riverbed.

Taking Action

1 dream I am
high-flying duck's eyes
over an ocean, washed
in fire-splash sunset.

I dream I am
two swimming shark's eyes
in search of swallowed
whole-fish dinner.

I dream we cross an open field
and face a lion in our track.
Making one group body, oddly, we
come together, thrusting arms like horns
and flapping our clothes like fighting
wings, while we scream in waves
like earsplitting sirens.
The lion turns and runs in terror.

I dream I am
color pieces of feelings
in music notes, jumping up
on the keys of a piano
playing it together.
I dream of a lot that puzzles me.

First Time I See Properly

First time I see God
we will do a great running on air together

Holding hands
God and me will do a burst
of running from my yard

Oh, how we lift up
over fences and walls
to settle running in space
effortless like walking
high over roads and telegraph wires
on and on over woods
over fields and bridges
over tops of houses
over hills up and down
passing streams and rivers

Recharged and recharged smoothly
on and on space running holding hands
we now have under us
only the wide and wider sea

We run and we run above the great water
while days and nights come and go
and more days and nights come and go
till down we arrive
landing
on a sandy beach
of different families of birds

How long we live here
we do not really know
We only know our joys
finding new foods and new fruits
and trying new ways to eat them
and acting out new and newer stories
and acting out more new and newer stories.

A Nest Full of Stars

Only chance made me come and find
my hen, stepping from her hidden
nest, in our kitchen garden.

In her clever secret place, her tenth
egg, still warm, had just been dropped.

Not sure of what to do, I picked up
every egg, counting them, then put them
down again. *All were mine.*

All swept me away and back.
I blinked, I saw: a whole hand
of ripe bananas, nesting.

I blinked, I saw: a basketful
of ripe oranges, nesting.

I blinked, I saw: a trayful
of ripe naseberries, nesting.

I blinked, I saw: an open bagful
of ripe mangoes, nesting.

I blinked, I saw:
a mighty nest full of stars.

naseberry: sapodilla plum with sweet brown flesh

Echoes of a Caribbean
School Playground

Caribbean Playground Song

Say, Good mornin, Granny Maama.
Good mornin, Granpa Taata.
  Good mornin when it rainin.
  Good mornin when sun shinin.
  Good mornin.

Say, Good mornin, Miss Pretty-Pretty.
Good mornin, one-yeye Mista Shorty.
  Good mornin when sun shinin.
  Good mornin when hurrikaanin.
  Good mornin.

Say, Good mornin, Mista Big-N-Fat Man.
Good mornin, Mista Maaga Man.
Good mornin when sun shinin.
Good mornin when hurrikaanin.
Good mornin.

Say, Good mornin, Mista Lamefoot.
Good mornin, dear Miss No-Toot.
Good mornin when sun shinin.
Good mornin when hurrikaanin.
Good mornin.

Say, Good mornin, dear-dear Bush Miss.
Good mornin, dear Mista Touris.
Good mornin when sun shinin.
Good mornin when hurrikaanin.
Good mornin.

Say, Good mornin, Granny Maama
Good mornin, Granpa Taata.
Good mornin.

one-yeye: one-eyed
Maaga: meager or thin
No-Toot: No-tooth
Bush Miss: someone who lives far from
        the village on woody land
Touris: Tourist

Swinging

You ride a swing out and back
trees ride with you up and down.

You ride a swing out and back
road rides with you up and down.

You ride a swing out and back
buildings ride with you up and down.

You ride a swing out and back
swinging world rides with you up and down.
      Swinging
            Oh, swinging
                  Swinging . . .

Smooth Skippin

Skip a-show groun is evva too hot.
Easy. Easy. Whether thin or fat
a-listn poor man rattle quatty
as him go on all chatty-chatty.

Skip betta than doin a frog jump.
Skip betta than droppin on yu rump—
a-listn ol lady at fireside
a-tell bout the prettiest bride
a-tell bout the prettiest bride
a-tell bout the prettiest bride . . .

a-show: showing
a-listn: listening
quatty: old coin worth about a penny
a-tell: telling

Old Men Called Arawak

'Cos he coughed, coughed, and choked
as he smoked, smoked, and smoked,
spitter man old Daddy Brock
got named Smoker Arawak.
             Got named Smoker Arawak.

'Cos he ate only best bammy
made by best-loved granny,
old man Mister Mack
got named Cassava Arawak.
             Got named Cassava Arawak.

Arawak: original natives of Jamaica
bammy: a flat Jamaican cassava bread
cassava: a root vegetable

He Loved Overripe Fruits

Hot sweaty body carrying treats,
my Caribbean grandpa came home,
turned his pockets inside out
and gave us runny, soft, sticky sweets.

Other times, the sweaty wet pockets
brought us bruised, overripe fruits
like bananas or blackberries

or, sometimes, mangoes, plums,
gineps, naseberries,
or a tempting mixture of these.

Other times we knew how
to push, tussle, compete hard
to take off Grandpa's boots.

Not always, but, often,
turned upside down, the boots
carried small change in them:
tipped out all round the floor,
as he smiled, seeing who got how much.

ginep: big-tree fruit, bunched like grapes;
    creamy flesh covers its pits
naseberry: sapodilla plum with sweet brown flesh

West Indian Boys
Play Village Cricket

Bowl ball, man. Bowl yu unplayable:
mek me hit it, man—
bash Englan stuck
in-a sun face.

Bowl ball. Bowl bad-man ball:
mek me crash Aussie
in-a moon side.

Bowl ball, man. Bowl yu fixer:
mek me strike Small Islan team
flyin to nex worl.

Aussie: Australians
fixer: gets the better of the opposition
Small Islan: one of the smallest Caribbean islands

Queen and King Mullet

King says, Queen Mullet, mam,
yu so prettily pinky white
Oh, I love yu lovely sight.
                    Oh, I love yu lovely sight.

Queen says, King Mullet, sar,
yu beard is right.
Oh, yu beard is jus, jus right.
                    Oh, yu beard is jus, jus right . . .

Mullet: goatfish variety with a pair of long barbels
        below the mouth like a beard

Donkey Story

This everywhere world that I have found
is no flat, straight, smooth, or level ground.

This place with little and big-big holes
is fixed with little and big-big stones.

You go on uphill, you go downhill
loaded, loaded, if you feel well or ill—
       loaded, loaded, if you feel well or ill. . . .

Doubtful Sayings

Take hot bad licks and nevva evva cry,
Yu'll give some back before yu die.

Eat a big bug and dohn cough it up,
jaws'll crack big nut with yu mouth shut.

Duppy eyes livin in a cut bamboo
will come to live in ragged ol shoe.

Dress in notn pretty and eat notn sweet,
duppy'll hol yu han as yu walk on street.

Eat yu food up fram pearl dishes,
yu'll ketch fish beyond all wishes.
      Yu'll ketch fish beyond all wishes. . . .

licks: blows
duppy: a ghost
ketch: catch

Duppy Dance

*Y*ou walk too-too late at night,
duppies make your wrong road the right.
Around you they rattle strings of bones.
    And duppies dance. Duppies dance.

All along deep-deep dark road,
duppies croak like huge hidden toad.
You hear distant scary bells toll.
    And duppies dance. Duppies dance.

Duppies make horses' hooves *clop-clop*.
Make some strange big birds flutter up.
Make you feel your skin gone shriveled.
    And duppies dance. Duppies dance.

Roaring, snorting, like ten bulls,
duppies rip off your clothes—one pull!
Skeletons prance all around you.
    And duppies dance. Duppies dance.

duppy: a ghost

Mysteries

My Laughable Drawings

In my artwork book
two drawings especially
tickle people.

Long faces drinking
at a water hole are
splayed-legs giraffes
taking up the whole picture.

All spreading thin legs
attach themselves
to a wiry body, with unruly
ears, and a pinched
cricket-bat face taking drink.

My next drawing looks as if
a house decorator's dirty
rag cloths—blobbed, smeared,
and streaked, with a rainbow
of colors—have got sewn together.

Then all a baggy, blowy show
my three dressed-up boys
look springy and bouncy
swinging along together, wearing
windblown flags of the world.

Getting Bigger Rap

*W*atch me getting bigger and bigger,
stepping wider, walking taller.

Nothing easier in a tussle,
but now I'm better when I whistle.

Barring, too, that only game called darts,
I know much of who is who in sports.

And though no worm with book-intake look,
I sometimes do know a latest book.

See me how my clothes are cut in style,
all ready to walk down the aisle.

See how more and more I'm on the ball,
and it's little bother if I fall.
   And it's little bother if I fall.

   Watch me getting bigger and bigger,
      stepping wider, walking taller higher,
         stepping wider, walking taller higher. . . .

Woods Whisperings

We woods whisper. We whisper:
You will find in us
whole naked families
of roofs, floors, beds, toothpicks,
chest of drawers, bats, walking sticks.

We woods whisper. We whisper:
You will find in us
naked mask families
of gods, devils, clowns,
and even faces of lions.

We woods whisper. We whisper:
You will find in us
whole naked families
of flutes, with one the bamboo,
one the deep-voiced didgeridoo.

We woods whisper. We whisper:
You will find in us
whole naked families
of carved girls and boys—
all faces of toys.

We woods whisper. We whisper:
You will find in us
whole naked families
of rocking horses.
We woods come and live in your houses.

Granddad's Visitor

*A*fter a good, big supper
Granddad dozed off
in his comfy chair.

Granddad woke to see
he had a sitting visitor
looking at him with a strange smile.

Granddad knew the visitor.
He smiled, saying, "Hello!"
Getting up, he moved toward

his visitor, stretching for
a handshake. Then horror
wiped away Granddad's smile.

No one was sitting there.
Puzzled, Granddad shuffled
back to his chair and sat.

Looking up, he saw
the visitor was still there.
He knew the visitor.

He got up again to greet
his visitor. As he turned
round, he saw only the chair.

Granddad stood awhile.
Then he sat down again.
When he looked up slowly,
no one was there.

Showman

See showman of the village.
See as he sings and dances,
how spiders and scorpions
and centipedes all crawl
from his pockets.

And slowly they climb up
to settle there, in his face.
And when he smiles, his
face comes newly alive
with crawling insects.

And when he grins, all try
to settle on his teeth, piling
up on top of each other. He
sings and dances again. All
move slowly back, into his pockets.

MISTER-RY

Wild New-Forest Pony takes my apple.
Eats my banana, too. Looks for more.
I stroke him. He follows me. So strangely
friendly toward me, he makes me
suddenly name him MISTER-RY. And more.
Next morning—shocks me out of bed.

Arched back with long legs and neck
crops grass, in our front garden. I
rush out calling MISTER-RY! MISTER-RY!
In a low rumble of a neigh, he comes—
long face pushing, nuzzling me.

Our dog, WORRIER, dashes about,
teasing MISTER-RY to play with him.
Picking him up, I put WORRIER lying
flat on the back of the horse. All
on his own he walks with dog rider
round and round the garden. Then, my go.

Holding neck and mane, I climb up,
sit erect, having my trotting ride
round the garden, when, along my
street side, a blast of applause shakes me
and goes on through my barebacked ride,
never stopping. I say, OK, MISTER-RY.

Sharp, sharp, he stops. I dismount,
looking. I see THE QUEEN. Clapping too,
THE QUEEN is there, saying to me,
Give him a drink now. Give him a drink.

I run into the house. Get a bucket
of water. Come back with it, panting
with new disbelief.

     No horse is there.
          No audience is there.
In the far, far distance I hear
wild clattering of hooves going,
     going away. . . .

Index of First Lines